Weather Wise

by Rebecca Weber

Content and Reading Adviser: Mary Beth Fletcher, Ed.D.
Educational Consultant/Reading Specialist
The Carroll School, Lincoln, Massachusetts

Spyglass
BOOKS

COMPASS POINT BOOKS

Minneapolis, Minnesota

Compass Point Books
3722 West 50th Street, #115
Minneapolis, MN 55410

Visit Compass Point Books on the Internet at *www.compasspointbooks.com*
or e-mail your request to *custserv@compasspointbooks.com*

Photographs ©: Two Coyotes Studio/Mary Foley, cover; Imagestate, 5, 7, 9, 11; TRIP, 6, 19;
PhotoDisc/Getty Images, 10; TRIP/H. Rogers, 13, 15; Robert Landau/Corbis, 14; TRIP/P. Barkham, 17;
TRIP/B. Turner, 18.

Project Manager: Rebecca Weber McEwen
Editor: Heidi Schoof
Photo Researcher: Image Select International Limited
Photo Selectors: Rebecca Weber McEwen and Heidi Schoof
Designer: Jaime Martens
Illustrator: Anna-Maria Crum

Library of Congress Cataloging-in-Publication Data

Weber, Rebecca.
  Weather wise / by Rebecca Weber.
     p. cm. — (Spyglass books)
Summary: Tells how to predict the weather using traditional expressions.
Includes bibliographical references and index.
  ISBN 0-7565-0385-X
  1. Weather—Juvenile literature. [1. Weather forecasting.] I. Title.
  II. Series.
  QC981.3 .W4295 2002
  551.6—dc21
                          2002002758

Contents

Rainy Weather

There are old *sayings* that can help you be weather wise.

"Red sky in the morning, sailor take warning." This means there will soon be rain.

Sunrise

This is true! If the sun looks red, there is a lot of dust in the air. As clouds form, water will gather around the dust and fall to the ground as rain.

Frosty Weather

There is an old saying about *frost.*
"Clear moon, frost soon."
This means there may be frost in the night.

The moon

This is true! If the moon and stars look clear, there isn't much *moisture* in the air to hold heat near Earth. If it gets cold enough, it will frost.

Frost

Windy Weather

There is an old saying about wind.
"*Mare's* tails and fish *scales* make tall ships take in their sails." This means it will be windy.

This is true! If the clouds up in the sky look wispy or look like fish scales, they are being blown by strong wind.

These clouds look like fish scales.

These clouds look
like a mare's tail.

Stormy Weather

There is an old saying about storms.
"*Halo* around the sun or moon, rain or snow will come soon." This means a cold, wet storm is coming.

The sun

17

This is true! If you see a bright ring around the sun or moon, you are looking at a thin cloud of *ice crystals.* These form before a storm.

The moon

More Old Sayings

If chickens eat in the rain, it will rain all day. If chickens wait in the **coop,** the rain will be over soon.

Seabirds, stay out from the land. We won't have good weather while you're on the sand.

Birds and bugs can predict a tornado.

Glossary

coop–a special building where chickens live

frost–frozen ice crystals that cover plants, buildings, and cars after a cold night

halo–a bright ring of light

ice crystal–a small, frozen piece of water

mare–a female horse

moisture–tiny drops of water

saying–something useful that people say often

scale–one of many small pieces of shiny, protective skin on a fish

Learn More

Books

Dussling, Jennifer. *Pink Snow and Other Weird Weather.* Ill. by Heidi Petach. New York: Grosset & Dunlap, 1998.

Fowler, Allan. *What Do You See in a Cloud?* New York, Childrens Press, 1996.

Rogers, Paul. *What Will the Weather Be Like Today?* Pictures by Kazuko. New York: Greenwillow Books, 1989.

Web Sites

sln.fi.edu/weather/index.html

www.crh.noaa.gov/mkx/owlie/owlie.htm

Index

GR: I
Word Count: 210

From Rebecca Weber

I grew up in the country, so I have always loved nature. I enjoy teaching people about the world and how to take care of it.